W9-AHX-746

"Our worldview affects every area of our lives. In **SHAPE**, Jesse James helps us see the world as it is not as we want it to be. Armed with this truth, we can live the life we were meant to live."

~ Mark Miller, VP Training and Development, Chick-fil-A; International best selling author, speaker and consultant

"Jesse James contributes greatly to the demolition of the fatal dualistic world view of sacred and secular. He lays out a pattern of thinking about our vocations that transforms work from merely an economic endeavor to a life giving redemptive process. A must read for all of us who draw a paycheck."

~ Mike Bell, CPA Co-Founder, Bell & Rhodes, PC; Edmond, Oklahoma

"Reading **SHAPE** provides one with a very practical way to incorporate the reality of a world view into daily life. We are all shaped by a world view. Jesse helps us to realize and embrace that fact as truth; a truth that leads to keen focus, to deep perspective and to future restoration. The Eight Principles discussed will help guide the reader in all aspects of life. I highly recommend this book for all people, but especially to those in positions of leadership."

~ Bill Bland, Senior Vice President, Choate Construction Company; Atlanta, Georgia

"I found **SHAPE** to be an extremely thought provoking journey that led to meaningful self reflection and a rededication to live life with an intentionality that makes a difference. The Eight Principles of **SHAPE** are revealed with a heavy dose of clarity and simplicity that will impact young and old alike. Jesse James has issued the challenge to write our life story with truth and to leave a legacy that is not measured by what we accomplish, but by how many lives we touch. I encourage all who read **SHAPE** to join me in embracing Jesse's challenge."

~Terry Johnson, Co-Founder,
Jeremiah Partners, LLC. Atlanta, Georgia

"This book distills the timeless universally wise principles that Jesse James and his teams have taught thousands in the former Soviet Union. There is much to learn and practice in these pages."

~Bush Nielsen, Shareholder, Reinhart Boerner
van Deuren s.c., Milwaukee, Wisconsin

"In a meaningful way of looking at life differently, Jesse gives you encouragement and hope by coming to you spiritually from a unique perspective."

~ Dennis Bishop, owner - Bishop Farms, McComb, Ohio;
Co-owner, Bishop-Kandal Rentals, Findlay, Ohio.
Professor, coach and advisor

"It has been a great pleasure to be so close to you while so far away. Every word, every sentence I read was like you telling me the stories personally, exactly the way I know you. It is truly a Jesse James book full of insights on how to live a meaningful life. Just as I would expect, it is great stuff."

~ Thomas Bungard, German friend and manager of a German Stock Exchange Company, Munich, Germany

GLOBAL LEADERSHIP

SHAPE

the Business of a
Meaningful Life

Jesse L. James

dustjacket

www.dustjacket.com

Dedication

To my life partner of 46 years and endlessly creative wife, Carolynn, who consistently and lovingly believes in my writing when I don't.

To the Reader

Human beings are choice makers. The choices we make have consequences. Some consequences are immediate, others far removed from the moment of choice. Choices we make and choices we choose not to make, or even don't know to make, all have consequences. History is a collection of the consequences of the choices of billions upon billions of people down through the centuries. In that sense, our choices matter, for they write history.

It is often not so much lack of knowledge or just generally 'not knowing' that is at issue. More often it is simply a matter of initiating the choice itself.

In the following pages we are introduced to eight familiar and truthful principles surrounded by stories. They are 'truthful' because they reflect how things are made to work. They are the 'shape' of reality. The manner in which they are presented may appear new but the concept itself will likely resonate with you. The choice is to make the principle, a practice. The stories serve to illustrate how real people in real world situations chose to creatively 'practice' a principle. Choosing to engage a principle with proper intellectual analysis in order to accurately display wise practices has consequences. There is, of course, the unique consequence of each individual situation. However, the overarching consequence of a life lived in concert with the 'shape' of reality is "the business of a meaningful life".

Wisdom implores us to think truthfully and live consciously. It is a choice.

Special Thanks

To my Global Leadership board who have patiently encouraged the writing of this book. Denny Bishop incentivized and provided a delightful writing environment in Panama City, Panama. Each board member in his own way provoked me to stay the course and complete the project; Mike Bell, Brad Yarbrough, Tom Gwaltney, Wayne Hoover, Rob Morris, Kurt Ling and Emery Shane. The generosity of spirit of each one in his own unique way contributed immeasurably to the completion of this writing journey.

Contents

The SHAPE of THINGS

His idea was worth hundreds of thousands of dollars. The computer models by some of the major farm implement companies demonstrated that it would not work. Rather than a computer model, he decided to create a prototype of the particular piece of equipment he had in mind. The idea was unique. It combined several functions (harvest-soil analyzation and replanting) into one piece of equipment, making it feasible to enter the field once and still accomplish three things. It would increase efficiency, save time and minimize damage to the field. The prototype clearly demonstrated that it did, indeed, work and the international manufacturing company made him an attractive offer. He said, "It isn't for sale." Then he continued, "You can have it for nothing!" He laughed with pleasure and delight when he told me the story. He loves life, encourages people and shares his agricultural ideas to enrich the lives of other farmers.

It isn't that he is independently wealthy and doesn't need the money. That isn't it at all. It is something in him that runs a lot deeper than a few more dollars. He loves business, has done well with it. He continues to be the quintessential entrepreneur—admired by all who know him, and I don't doubt a little bit envied by a few. Whether it's his real estate business, manufacturing, farming, investing or inventing, he possesses an assumption about life that is easily missed by the casual observer. Identifying that assumption is the subject of this book.

It's curious to me that Denny is seventy and still dreaming; still pleasuring in offering others a leg up. He adds new meaning to the concept of generosity. It is a generosity that goes well beyond dollars. It's deeper than that. Anyone can give dollars. Giving one's life is another matter. In conversation one day he lamented growing older, not so much for reasons of aging, but because he has another lifetime of dreams and ideas to share. To him "age" is only an indicator that time is running out on being able to see all his visions become reality. I watched his eyes light up, and I listened as the rhythm of his voice quickened with excitement. At a time when many are thinking of retiring and indulging, Denny's still very much in the game . . . and his story continues.

And then I think of Jake. I knew him for forty-three years. I don't remember much of what he ever said. He didn't talk much. But in the years since his death, hardly a week has gone by that I don't reflect on his life in some manner. Often it's nothing more than a fleeting thought, triggered by something I see or hear. What Jake was outlived him. I remember his presence and his simple desires. I recall his laugh . . . and his pipe—it always protruded from his lips behind which was a frequent Cheshire smile . . . and a twinkle in his eye.

He worked hard in his business of farming. He respected people and honored animals, especially his horses. When he grew too old to manage his land, he leased it to his neighbors. The often-heard comment made by everyone who knew him was, "You can take a handshake from Jacob Rose to the bank." When a deal was made with Jake, a handshake would seal it. Only as I grew older did I begin to realize the unfolding implications of that statement. It revealed a man underneath a weathered exterior who added up to something that outlived him. The mystery for me was the "something." What exactly was that?

He worked hard, but a lot of people work hard. He was content with his simple life with no indoor plumbing or phone. His two-room house was much smaller than the barn in which his animals lived. He possessed a deep sensitivity for the environment before it was politically correct to do so. However, none of that seems to equal his "presence" that remains with me and others who knew him. What stays with me is far more than the sum total of a list of things I can remember about my grandfather. The phrase, "What I am outlives what I say" comes to mind. It's the "I am" part that causes me to ponder my grandfather's life, as well as Denny's.

What is that 'something' in Denny that runs deeper than a few more dollars? What is that 'presence' of my grandfather that sticks with me and others? What is it that seems to have provided 'meaning' far beyond the acquisition of a few more things or accomplishments? This is the subject of exploration of this book.

There are a plethora of wonderfully helpful books on the market that address keys to leadership and steps to success—in both life and business. Many wisely purchase these books and apply the information to their particular situation. It is often the case, however, that when we add up the sum totals of all the parts contained in these books something seems to be missing. It's not that the books contain bad information because they don't. It's just that there's more to it than steps and techniques or processes and formulas.

There is an observable commonality and it surfaces as what I would call "attitude". It can also be described as the "assumptions" about life a person holds that are derived from a particular worldview. This would include the very broad and overarching areas of life such as a person's view of work, life, love, human beings, religion and family. Each of us has a specific set of assumptions through which we view all of these things and more. Whether we are consciously aware of the assumptions is another matter. And this is part of the commonality that was referred to earlier. Some people possess the conscious awareness and ability to articulate the way the present world is seen. Living consciously seems to be a part of their profile.

A simple illustration will clarify this concept. I have worn glasses most of my life. I was in high school the first time a pair of corrective lenses ever came between my eyes and my view of the world. I had no idea the assumptions I had formed about the world around me. My glasses changed all that. The eye doctor told me to take a few minutes to get used to the new sensation of the corrective lenses.

I will never forget looking out the office window, across the street to a small grove of trees. I could see the leaves—each leaf! Prior to this moment, it had never occurred to me that I was simply seeing "green."

With my new glasses I could see a distinction within the shades of green. At first it was difficult to get used to. It was even somewhat uncomfortable, and I wasn't even sure I liked it. It didn't take long, however, for those thoughts to go away as I sat in that chair in the doctor's office. I liked the clarity and definition a correct set of lenses provided. No longer was I viewing the world in a distorted manner. I was viewing it as it really is. The key to all of this is having a correct set of lenses.

We live life according to the way we see the world, whether we are aware of it or not. I had no idea how negatively influenced my school experience was before I received my corrective lenses. A worldview that works—one that fits the "shape of reality"—will resonate with the way we experience life and business on a daily basis. There will be little to no conflict of substance. It influences the manner in which we live, informs the choices we make and provides the satisfaction and meaning we desire in life. My use of the term "shape" is a metaphor to explain how things work or possess definition.

Consider a colony of ants as a simple illustration of "shape." Most of us ignore ants until they get into our living space and become a nuisance. We see them as an everyday part of life, scattered here and there. We don't really spend any time thinking about ants unless we require the services of a pest control professional. A good professional is very aware that there is a structure and definition in a colony of ants. The ants trail each other by following a scent; there are defined work assignments and a very observable pattern in the behavior of a colony.

The professional employs this knowledge of the "shape" of reality in the world of ants to effectively apply his services. This is a very small example (pun intended) of how I am using the idea of "shape." The world in which we live is made to work a certain way with corresponding consequences. It's how life works. Like the ant colony, whether we're aware of it or not, there is definite order, structure, pattern and definition (shape) to reality.

Our view of the world around us and the assumptions we hold are not something with which we are born. They are developed, learned and cultivated in the context of our life experiences, both formally and informally. They include our family of origin, religious culture, movies and books, education, personal experiences and the national/political culture in which we live. Our view of the world is a very complex collection of ideas, concepts, beliefs and values we form over time. They are "assumptions" because we really are unaware of them. They are just present, behind the scenes of our thinking, usually unexamined and very much like the default settings of a computer. Cultivating our worldview is a lifelong journey.

An extreme, and in this case, very sad illustration of this phenomenon is the 1994 movie, Nell. Though the character is fictional, the story was based on a 1992 play called Idioglossia, written by an American playwright/screenwriter Mark Handley. Nell was approximately thirty years old when she was discovered living in the backwoods of North Carolina. She was raised by a mother who suffered from a stroke, leaving her unable to speak without a significant slur in her speech. Nell had a twin sister who died as a young girl.

Nell was kept from any contact with the outside world. Her only human connection was her mother, who was now dead. Suddenly, Nell was alone and completely unaware of any reality outside her own experience. She invented her own "idioglosstic" language(based on the play's name, Idioglossia) which she created from mimicking her mother's slurred speech.

The movie follows the journey of two people, Jerry and Natasha, who are assigned by the court to integrate Nell into society. Her journey is marked with fear, wonder and anxiety as she discovers the world as it really is, rather than how she had seen it for so many years. After five years of hard work, the movie ends on a positive note for Nell as she warmly and successfully embraces an objective reality—still remembering from where she had come.

Our view of the world around us and the assumptions we hold are not necessarily good or bad; they just are what they are. However, in the case of Nell, we would have to agree it was bad and sad. The question that surfaces is one posed earlier, and that is, "Do I have the correct set of lenses?" This is important because there really is an objective reality. Trees do have leaves and those leaves have size, shape, texture, and color variations. It matters that one views reality as it objectively exists.

The first time I met Inna, September 2001, she was somewhat guarded and distant. She was a department head at her University, an expert in Shakespearian literature, very professional and excellent at her task of interpreting for our seminar. One year later, in September 2002, she again interpreted for us. This time, something changed in her, evidenced by her comments, "These three days were unforgettable, and I still feel the drive inside me which was left by the seminar. Thank you for sharing the "right lenses" with me. I keep asking myself what my life would have been like had I not met you and your team. I clearly see the difference. I am counting the days when you will return again."

Her reference to the "right lenses" came directly from interpreting my worldview comments during the seminar. I was making the point that our unconscious set of assumptions with which we view life is like the lenses of a pair of glasses. When we view life through the lenses of our worldview, we organize our impressions of what we see and experience accordingly. That being the case, it is important we have the correct "lenses;" otherwise we are going to see reality in a distorted manner rather than as it really is. Of course, a person can live indefinitely with distortion. However, over time, it greatly diminishes the richness and meaning of the kind of life one experiences.

One of the ironies for me concerning this encounter with Inna was the location of the seminar venue. We met in a room on the second floor of a building overlooking Karl Marx Avenue. History records Karl Marx as the co-founder of Marxism and the author of *The Communist Manifesto* and *Das Kapital*—materialist conception of history. At the end of Karl Marx Avenue was a large and looming statue of Vladimir Ulyanov (Lenin), Prime Minister of the USSR. Both men represent ideologies responsible directly and indirectly for the deaths of millions. Inna is a classic example of what happens when worldviews collide—one truthful, one false.

The people of the former USSR countries are characterized by a desperate need for a guiding worldview, or "soul food" as stated by Perry Glanzer in his book, *The Quest for Russia's Soul*. "Because the regime was captive to its own lies, it had to falsify everything. It falsified the past. It falsified the present and the future. It falsified statistics . . . it pretended to respect human rights. It pretended to persecute no one. It pretended to fear no one. It pretended to pretend nothing. (Vaclav Havel 1987, pg. 58)

"In addition to a legacy of falsification, devotion to Lenin ran deep. It went far beyond encouraging emulation of his moral qualities. It also had a religious quality. Shrines and icons to Lenin could be found in numerous schools. Shrines to Lenin could be found in almost every kindergarten classroom. Each room would have a portrait of Lenin surrounded by fresh flowers and ribbons usually placed on a small table beneath the picture. In 1978 a popular music book was published for school children with a rousing tribute to Lenin: 'Lenin is always alive, Lenin is always with you, in sorrow, hope and joy. Lenin is in your spring, in every happy day. Lenin is in you and me. Lenin is now more alive than the living'" (Dunstan, 1993, p.167).

Helen, an English teacher from Rybinsk, Russia, summed up the feelings of many,". . . I cannot trust the newspapers. Not just me, but everybody cannot trust our papers because we were told that Lenin was the best person in life. He was the best person. Then we were told that Stalin was very good, and he did a lot of good things for the people. Then we learned the truth that it was not so. Then we learned not very good things about our life from our newspapers. Then we learned that some of our newspapers did not tell us the truth. So in order to know everything, in order to think of our future, we should know the truth. Sometimes we can't trust our papers; sometimes we can't trust our government, our authority. This is the thing. Not just me, but all of us. Sometimes we can't trust our authorities; sometimes we can't trust our friends; and sometimes we can't trust our husbands and wives. Everyone can betray you."

When Boris Yeltsin was the president of Russia, I led a team of American educators to Russia to a city called, Chita. I met a woman in Chita who served as his deputy in that region, representing the interests of the Kremlin. Her entire life represented a kind of learned distrust. Being suspicious of everyone was a significant part of her life assumption. Her "job" was to be suspicious. She demonstrated it well upon our first meeting as she made it very clear she did not like or appreciate our presence in Chita and that the day of our departure would be a good day.

However, she had a middle school daughter, named Katya. Katya liked us right away and chose to hang around us as much as she could. Like any child, she was curious, engaging and full of questions. Her mom softened quickly as she observed our kindness toward her daughter, as well as Katya's delight with her new-found friends. Her suspicion faded and trust grew. The world she had been taught to distrust was not the real world at all. Our relationship grew, time passed and eventually Katya came to the United States to live with us as we were able to get her enrolled in a University in Indiana. Katya's mom was able to see through the eyes of her own daughter the error of her worldview. The assumptions with which we live merit conscious examination. The consequences can be quite determinative.

I met Larissa in the city of Yoshkar-Ola in the Russian republic of Mari-El. It was the mid-1990's, so it had not been long since the official demise of the USSR. My team of educators was greeted with the mixed emotions of curiosity and fear. Not only were we the first Americans to ever set foot in their city, but we were staying for a week in a local hotel—conducting seminars with several hundred of their educators.

The initial reaction to our arrival? Our plane was met with military personnel, and we were told to get back on the plane and go home. We were not welcome. My reaction was, "NO." We went to a lot of trouble to get there, and we were not about to go back home. The next day I met with the president of the Mari-El Republic, and he decided we could stay as long as he could assign some people to attend our seminar.

The seminar went as planned. Larissa was with the KGB and her assigned job was to be my "assistant." Of course, we both knew what was going on. However, her constant vigilance and attempts to somehow discredit our presence gave way to a growing curiosity within her, along with an awareness that we meant no harm. All she ever knew in her young twenty-plus years of life was distrust. It was her job, her pattern of thinking, and it was her basic relational assumption. Larissa approached everything she did largely without even recognizing that distrust was present in her every thought. When the week was over and it was time to go home, she said her goodbyes to us through tears.

During that week with us she observed an alternative and she was changing. I told her I knew what her job was that week and that she had failed; and I hoped she didn't get fired. She smiled and said it didn't matter anymore to her. She was quickly realizing that the world she thought was real was not the real world at all. She had been operating with a set of distorted assumptions her entire young life, but now that was changing.

Sociologically speaking, the Russian people have experienced what Emile Durkheim and Peter Berger describe as individual and collective "anomie."

(Berger, 1969, pg. 22) "....describes 'anomie' as radical separation from a socially constructed world of knowledge. In cases of individual and collective 'anomie,' the fundamental order in terms of which the individual can 'make sense' of his life and recognize his own identity will be in process of disintegration. Not only will the individual begin to lose his moral bearings, with disastrous psychological consequences, but he will become uncertain about his cognitive bearings as well. The world begins to shake . . . "

This is an extreme example to be sure, but it is still very illustrative of the importance and significance of a person's worldview. Since 1986 I have come to know many in the former USSR whose experience was very similar to the "anomie" description . . . with varying extremes.

Sometimes our assumptions can be amusing. A young interpreter sat with an American friend and me, listening to us talk. She asked how far away from each other we lived. I said about ten minutes, depending on the time of day. Later in the week she learned we lived about eight miles from each other. She was puzzled. She didn't understand how one could walk eight miles in ten minutes. She was thinking "walking"—we were thinking "driving." It's a little thing that makes for a fun story to tell, but it illustrates the point of how important it is to be conscious of our assumptions when we're attempting to communicate with one another. Her assumption and life experience were not resonating with the concept of driving.

We live in a world that has objective shape/definition. Things work a certain way because they are hardwired to work in that manner. How we view the world does not change reality. How we view the world will determine how well and effectively we engage life and work.

The SHAPE of EIGHT

Our basic responsibility as human beings is to live truthfully—to live in a manner consistent with the shape of reality. Failing to do so has an eventual corresponding natural consequence. Wise is the one who seeks to understand the shape of reality and then to live accordingly. Saul of Tarsus was his Jewish name. He was born and lived in the first century. Largely due to his Roman citizenship and his conversion to Christianity, he is more historically known today as Paul the apostle. He traveled throughout what we know today as Greece, Syria, Malta and Turkey. In his letter to a group of Christians in Galatia (Turkey), he responded to the insistence of some that they perform up to a specific external list of "do's and don'ts" in order to make God happy.

Paul vigorously contested this assumption with two representative lists of characteristics and behaviors. One list flows out of what he calls the "sinful (broken) nature" and the other list flows out of God's spirit. The first list focuses more on what comes naturally to us, and the second list is about choosing to govern yourself, to monitor your thoughts and deeds. The latter list works the best in both life and society because it's how things are made to work—the shape. The "broken" list explains why we don't have to teach our children to misbehave; it comes naturally. Of course it does, and that's why parents try to teach the wisdom of making moral and ethical choices in life and work.

The "spirit"' list is about self-governing and as such diminishes the need in a society for laws. How silly it would be to have a law against being too kind, or too self-controlled, etc. However, the more a society is characterized by the first list, the more necessary it is to impose rules. Laws enforce a measure of acceptable civility in order to live satisfying and productive lives. Paul's point is that God is already "happy with us."

The objective is to live our lives consistently with the shape of reality. It's just a smarter and more productive way to live. It works. It makes sense to do what works. It's not a religious issue; it's a practical issue.

The past twenty-two-plus years of working, living and traveling in a culture quite juxtaposed to my own has deeply informed and transformed my thinking. I have observed the official demise of a Soviet-driven communist socialist structure. I have watched their attempt to embrace democracy and engage in commerce as a capitalist system. It has been revealing, indeed. Capitalism without a conscience and capitalism with a conscience are two entirely different things. The West has become the financial engine of the world— not so much because of capitalism, but because of the "conscience" that generally characterizes the capitalism of the West.

Capitalism that is not based on the foundation to live truthfully becomes an effective agent of greed and exploitation. Capitalism is not destructive in and of itself. It becomes destructive when individuals choose to engage in commerce in a manner devoid of moral and ethical principles. It's easier and less threatening to blame a system rather than to take individual responsibility for the choices I make. As Paul described in Galatians, it is the assumption of a conscience deeply informed by a moral and ethical perspective that drives success and provides meaning.

I began my comments talking about Denny, Jake, Nell, Inna and Larissa. Their experiences, cultures and countries of origin are very different, to be sure. However, I would suggest they share an observable commonality I would call a 'world view'. It's not the same one, of course, but they do each have one as do you and I. I've spent a lot of time in many countries but most of my focus is in the former USSR countries. My first exposure was a month long trip to Russia, Ukraine, Belarus and Georgia in 1986 and scores of trips since then. I mention this because I have observed the same commonality everywhere; we all possess a 'world view' that deeply informs our lives.

I have drawn some conclusions and made some observations during my years of engaging the post-Soviet culture. It continues to be informative and instructive to be so close to an emerging democracy and a fledgling capitalism. Life and work go well and produce effectively when there are certain assumptions that are operating in the background . . . like virus software. We will discuss eight principles which I believe work together to give conscience to capitalism and meaning to our life and work. This isn't rocket science and it isn't even new. However, working with hundreds of business and community leaders in the post-Soviet culture over the last couple of decades has caused me to reaffirm and assert certain truths.

These principles are always present where life thrives, businesses prosper and society is healthy. They are what contribute to the worldview of the individual. They are the collective assumptions of a society and the conscience of a free market system. I also assert they are universal principles in the sense that they are applicable everywhere. No nation or culture has a claim to ownership of them. How we choose to label a particular principle is not nearly as important as the operative truth of the principle itself. Neither is the order of these principles significant. One principle does not take priority over the others. What's important is to be aware of the principle and to assess how operative it is in your life and work. It's also important to determine the intentionality with which you choose to integrate it in your daily life.

These principles are reflective of how we view and value two things—human beings and work. Is a human being a cog on a wheel in a mechanistic universe? Or, is he created in the image of a Master Designer/Creator? Is one's value intrinsic to being human, or is value utilitarian? Is work a necessary evil in order to eat; or is work something more than simply earning a living?

The PRINCIPLE
of RECIPROCITY

This principle is rather intuitively familiar to each of us. It's called *reciprocity*. It is commonly referred to as the golden rule. The Judeo-Christian literature references it as "treating others the same way one would like to be treated." Still others describe it as "everything that goes around comes around." Again, the point of the principle is the *truth* of it—not how we say it. I will employ the concept of *reciprocity* for my discussion purposes and define it as "treating others in a manner one would enjoy being treated themselves."

The young lady worked at the small airport doing just about everything—including fueling the many private planes that stopped by daily on their long journeys across the United States. This particular day she serviced Lin's plane. She was kind, attentive and professional. Her job done, Lin tipped her generously and then he and his co-pilot taxied onto the tarmac and were airborne in a few minutes.

Two things you need to understand about Lin: One is his uncanny ability to accurately size up people, and two, his desire to give deserving young people a "leg up" in life—whatever that may look like. He wondered why she was working there and not going to school. He noticed her teeth needed some attention. These were not judgments, simply observations indicative of a possible need. He had his executive assistant find out more about her. Eventually Lin followed up with an offer of free orthodontic and dental care; and later he offered to fund her education at a local technical college she always wanted to attend—neither of which she could afford on her own. Astonished, shocked and almost unbelievingly she accepted this "no strings attached" offer.

Treating other people the way we would like to be treated is a choice. Lin could have easily given her a tip and that would have been that, but he chose not to simply give her a tip . . . and here's why. When Lin was thirteen years old someone took the time to give him a leg up. He started a business which grew to be one of the largest of its kind in the United States, active in almost every state. Passing the million and multi-million marks in his business never changed him as he continued to exercise *reciprocity*. It is this author's view that part of the reason for Lin's success lies in his frequent choice to wisely exercise this principle. Anyone who knows Lin can tell you many stories of his creativity in treating people the way he would like to be treated. It's a choice that usually costs the giver something; at the very least, the effort to engage.

It is upon this principle of reciprocity that the concept of customer service is based. The assumption is that we treat one another in this manner because human beings have value. Human beings have value because they are created beings; they are not cogs on a wheel in a mechanistic universe.

Value and worth is intrinsic to being human. Customer service is not a clever way to manipulate a potential customer into a place from which we can extricate a dollar or some other form of gain for ourselves. Rather, it is a choice to act into the life of another in a way that makes a difference to them. It's a choice to make a difference—one life at a time.

He was taking his usual early morning walk on the beach when in the distance he saw an older man walking toward him. As he approached the older man, he observed him picking up something and throwing it into the surf. As he drew closer his curiosity grew as he realized the older man was picking up starfish stranded on the beach by the tide and was throwing them back into the sea. He asked, "Sir, why do you take the time to throw starfish back into the sea?" The older man explained that if he didn't they would die on the beach in the morning sun. "But there are thousands of starfish on hundreds of beaches. How can you possibly make a difference?" The older man bent down, picked up another starfish and threw it into the surf and said, "It made a difference to that one" (by Loren Eiseley).

It becomes a choice to do for one person what we cannot do for everyone. Customer service and the principle of *reciprocity* fit like a hand in a glove. Customers are people who come into our store to purchase a product or service. They are, also, people who work with and for us. Thinking only of the person outside of our company as the customer is a one-dimensional definition of the term. Lin has an employee, named Neal, living in another city across the country who is married with children. One of those children is pre-school age and dyslexic. Upon discovering this, Lin asked his assistant to research special schools for such children. Properly handled early in life, one can manage quite well being dyslexic and Lin knew this from experience. The school was identified, happily in the same city as the family lived, and Lin's executive assistant notified them accordingly. Of course, the family was aware of the school but they also were aware it was extremely expensive, so they knew they were unable to take advantage of it. "You don't understand," replied the assistant, "there is no financial obligation to you. It is paid in full." The mother cried tears of joy in the midst of her overwhelming surprise. And, again, no strings attached. Nothing owed, no salary docked and no company commitment was required. Lin wisely knows his employee is also his customer.

Reciprocity is a choice. It requires thoughtful and creative consideration. Daily we should ask ourselves, "What does reciprocity look like in this particular situation?" What it looks like will vary from one time to another, one person to another and one situation to another. Therein is the fun and adventure of reciprocity. It's not boring, because it requires that we think creatively.

I can relate story after story of what it looks like for Lin and his company. But that is unique to Lin. One can easily dismiss all this because he has money and is able to do all these generous and wonderful things. If that is where we end up in our thinking, we have missed the point. There would be no story—if Lin did not possess a commitment to reciprocity. A lot of people have money, but no story . . . and it does not take money to have a story.

My wife and I have a favorite restaurant we frequent. The culture of the business at this particular location is reflective of our discussion and illustrated by a specific incident. One of the servers was involved in a serious automobile accident, resulting in extensive injuries that necessitated he be airlifted to the hospital. During his several days in the intensive care unit of the hospital, he had a steady stream of visitors—fellow servers and friends.

When released from the hospital many of the servers created a shift schedule to insure he was taken care of with regularity and that meals would be provided. The schedule included taking turns to stay overnight, sleeping on the floor to provide care. This responsibility involved months of attention and rehabilitation. These are kids who don't have money, but they do have a story. Certainly money would serve to expand their options, but it does not provide the story.

Choosing to put ourselves into another person's shoes is counter-intuitive. Taking the time and effort to ask myself how others look at me, my company or organization will reap great dividends. Once discovered, however, I have a choice to make. A very ancient proverb informs us, "To know the right thing to do and then to fail to do it is the greatest form of cowardice." Therein is the difference. Knowing isn't doing. Choosing to do the daily work of asking the question is the difference. What does *reciprocity* look like in this situation, that relationship or today's business transaction?

Several of our Ukrainian and Russian friends call the United States "customer service paradise." We have had many conversations about how and why our culture developed this attitude in business and the part this principle plays in it. A young Ukrainian surgeon and his wife stayed with us for several weeks preceding the Christmas holidays. Our outside decorations were up ..

. and rather extensive. Later in the evening before going to bed he offered to help me bring in the decorations for overnight, assuming that was my habit. I told him I left the decorations outside all month, and I would take them down in early January. He was amazed that no one would steal them. In his country he couldn't do anything like that because they would be taken. Yet another example of what we Americans take for granted—never taking the time to ponder why it is the way it is.

Making the choice to treat a human being with dignity and respect reveals an assumption concerning the value of a human being. In time the assumption permeates a culture and becomes an intuitive part of every decision made.

A friend of mine retired from Proctor and Gamble Corporation after spending his working lifetime with them. His job included overseeing the shutting down of plants from time to time. The company went to great lengths to be sure all employees were treated well financially. They also helped to find other jobs and even did some retraining. Why? Organizationally, it is the principle of *reciprocity* at work. I'm not suggesting everyone goes away happy and satisfied. I am suggesting that when *reciprocity* becomes a part of company culture, an effort is made to treat people well.

"Truth" has no agenda; as such, truth by its very nature has a freeing effect on us. There is an almost self-evident dimension to truth when we encounter it. It is not "propositional" truth so much that I am discussing as "truthful" living. A truthful view of "life" and "work" resonates with life experience. It's intuitive to us. Nancy Pearcey, in her wonderful book, Total Truth, discusses this very well and the origins of why this is so very true. She references some very ancient Judeo-Christian literature which informs us as to the beginnings, Genesis, of the creative order. The following both quotes and paraphrases her on this subject area. I give Mrs. Pearcey great credit for the impact her writing has had on me. I highly recommend you read her book for a broader discussion of this subject.

Genesis records God's original purpose in creating the human race. With the entrance of sin, humans went off course, lost their way, wandered off the path. But when we accept Christ's salvation, we are put back on the right path and are restored to our original purpose, resuming the task for which the human being was created.

And what is that task? In Genesis, God gives what we might call the first job description: "Be fruitful and multiply and fill the earth and subdue it." The first phrase, "be fruitful and multiply," means to develop the social world; build families, churches, schools, cities, governments, laws. The second phrase, "subdue the earth," means to harness the natural world; plant crops, build bridges, design computers, compose music. This is sometimes called The Cultural Mandate because it informs us that our original purpose as human beings was to create cultures and build civilizations.

This means that our vocation or professional work is not a second class activity. It is not something we do to just put food on the table. It is more than that. It is a high calling for which we were originally created. The way we serve a Creator God is by being creative with the talents and gifts He has given us. We could even say that we are called to actually continue God's own creative work.

Of course, we cannot create out of nothingness as did God. Our job is to develop the powers and potentials built into creation – using wood to build houses, cotton to make clothes, or silicon to make computer chips. Though modern social and economic institutions are not explicitly referred to, their justification is rooted in the Cultural Mandate.

In the first six days of the creation narrative in Genesis, God forms, then fills the physical universe – the sky with the sun and moon, the sea with swimming creatures, the earth with land animals and so on. Then the narrative *pauses, as though to emphasize that the next step will be the culmination of everything that went before. For the first time in His creative process, God announces His plan ahead of time; the members of the Trinity consult with one another: "Let us make a creature in our image who will represent us and carry on our work on earth" (Gen. 1:26). Then the first human couple is created and given dominion over the earth and to govern in God's name. This is delegated authority. They are to "cultivate" the earth, a word that has the same root as "culture."*

The way we express the image of God is by being creative and building cultures.

This was God's purpose when He originally made human beings and it remains His purpose today. His original plan was not withdrawn or made null and void by the Fall. Every aspect of human nature has been distorted and broken, but it has not made us less than human. We are not animals. We still reflect our original nature as God's image bearers. Even a person who does not believe in God still carries the Cultural Mandate. They multiply and fill the earth – which is to say they get married, have kids, raise families, start schools, run businesses and so on. They also cultivate the earth in that they fix cars, write books, study nature and invent new gadgets.

The Fall did not destroy our original calling. It made it more difficult. Our work is now marked by sorrow and hard labor. In Genesis 3:16 and 17, the Hebrew uses the word 'labor' as the same word for childbearing and also the 'labor' of growing food. Basically, the text informs us that the two major tasks in adult life of raising the next generation and making a living will be full of pain and disappointment because the world is fallen and fractured. All of our efforts will meet with the resistance and misdirection of our own selfishness and brokenness.

The lesson of the Cultural Mandate is that our sense of fulfillment depends on engaging *in creative, constructive work. The ideal human existence is expending creative effort which honors God and benefits others. We are called to cultivate the earth. Redemption is not a reference limited to establishing a relationship with God. It means entering upon a lifelong quest to devote our skills and talents to building things that are beautiful and useful, while at the same time resisting the distorting influence of a broken creation. Being a Christian means embarking on a lifelong process of growth in grace, both in our personal lives and in our vocations.*

Each of us has a role to play in cultivating the creation and working out God's norms for a just and humane society. Our vocation is not something we do for God, which would put a terrible burden on us to achieve and perform. Instead, it is a way of participating with God. God Himself engaged in not only the 'work' of salvation but also the 'work' of preserving and maintaining His creation.

You and I can make a significant difference within our own sphere of influence. However, along the way it necessitates making the daily choice to resist our craving for success, power, public acclaim and all else that is self-promoting and ultimately self-defeating. How we view life and work is profoundly determinative to what treating a human being with dignity and respect looks like through the uniqueness of our individual life.

We were conducting a business seminar in the beautiful port city of Odessa, Ukraine. Seven business men and women were on our team and an interpreter was assigned to each. Scott was assigned to an 18-year-old interpreter named Sasha. She had an excellent grasp of English and made it clear to us (in a nice way) that she was there to simply do the job and earn some dollars. The day began and Scott, a NASA scientist, treated her as respectfully as his own daughter. She politely listened to the presentations and assisted Scott in communication around his discussion table, when it was appropriate.

During one of the presentations Scott leaned over

to her and whispered into her ear to take notes in the manual provided, because one day she would likely use the material. Out of respect for Scott, she did so. Scott had no idea what he had just unlocked in her life. Each year, for the next five years, we returned to Odessa with different teams—conducting seminars with different business audiences. In the fifth year, a young lady walked up to me and asked if I remembered her. My memory of her returned as she referenced Scott and unfolded the story. Five years later she came to the seminar to find Scott and to tell him he had changed her life. I asked her how that was the case and she said, "He was the first person who ever believed in me. I came to find him and thank him. Today I am a successful business woman." The principle of reciprocity is certainly operative in this incident. At the very least, Scott treated Sasha the way he would want to be treated had the roles been reversed—with great dignity and respect as a human being with gifts and talents.

The PRINCIPLE of USE

Also operative in this story is the principle of use—as in "use it or lose it!" That's the short version of the idea, but it includes the larger picture of finding the "sweet spot" in one's own life and developing it. Our first priority, by necessity, is that we recognize and accept the fact of our uniqueness. This is a choice each of us makes.

It also relates to recognizing what another person does well, their sweet spot, and doing what one can do to grow, develop and encourage it. Scott observed the seed of something in Sasha and simply encouraged her with words. In her case that was all she needed to *use* and develop her unique "sweet spot." We cannot be really effective at helping another person if we are not growing ourselves. It's a parallel principle. Developing ourselves (*use* it before we lose it) goes hand in hand with engaging in the lives of others and developing them. When I assume the "mindset" of self-development, I am more likely to observe another person's passion and encourage their development as well. Because the principle of use is operative in my own life, I will more readily see and employ it in the life of another. If I happen to be in a supervisory position I can do even more to influence and create an environment for my co-worker's growth.

The founder of Chick-fil-A Corporation, Truett Cathy, makes the point very well when he often says, "Take care of people and people will take care of you." However, the taking care of people part is not something one does in a manipulative manner in order to extract a certain desired end or make dollars for the company. The motive is far more authentic, for it assumes an intrinsic value placed on the human being simply because they are a human being. The fact of value being gained for the company is a consequence of the principle, not the motivation for it. The motive is a question each of us answers for ourselves; in time, however, our motive will become apparent.

It's important to remember that these principles do not stand alone. There is a kind of ebb and flow with each of them as we choose to live our lives intentionally and consciously. One principle does not necessarily stand out over another in terms of importance, but the occasion tends to determine which principle rises to the forefront.

Author and communicator Tony Campolo tells a story about a boy named Teddy Stallard in his book, *Who Switched the Price Tags?* The story displays this principle of *use* quite well, and it also speaks volumes concerning the first principle of *reciprocity*. This story concerns a school teacher named Miss Thompson and her choice to engage with great intentionality in the life of one of her students. This is what it looked like in her life and workplace.

Teddy Stallard certainly qualified as "one of the least." Disinterested in school; musty, wrinkled clothes and hair never combed. One of those kids in school with a deadpan face, expressionless sort of a glassy, unfocused stare. When Miss Thompson spoke to Teddy, he always answered in monosyllables. Unattractive, unmotivated and distant, he was just plain hard to like. Even though his teacher said she loved all in her class the same, down inside she wasn't being completely truthful.

Whenever she marked Teddy's papers, she got a certain perverse pleasure out of putting X's next to the wrong answers, and when she put the F's at the top of the papers, she always did it with a flare. She should have known better; she had Teddy's records and she knew more about him than she was willing to admit. The record read:

> 1st grade: *Teddy shows promise with his work and attitude, but poor home situation.*
>
> 2nd grade: *Teddy could do better. Mother is seriously ill. He receives little help at home.*

3rd grade: *Teddy is a good boy, but too serious.*
He is a slow learner. His mother died last year.

4th grade: *Teddy is very slow, but well-behaved.*
His father shows no interest.

Christmas came and the boys and girls in Miss Thompson's class brought her Christmas presents. They piled their presents on her desk and crowded around to watch her open them. Among the presents was one from Teddy Stollard. She was surprised he had brought her a gift, but he did. Teddy's gift was wrapped in brown paper and was held together by scotch tape. On the paper were written the simple words, "For Miss Thompson from Teddy." When she opened Teddy's present, out fell an ugly bracelet with half the stones missing and a bottle of unattractive perfume.

The other boys and girls began to giggle and laugh over Teddy's gift, but Miss Thompson at least had enough sense to silence them by immediately putting on the bracelet and putting some of the perfume on her wrist. Holding her wrist up for the children to smell, she said, "Doesn't this smell lovely?" And the children taking their cue from the teacher, readily agreed with "oohs" and "ah's."

At the end of the day, when school was over and the other children had left, Teddy lingered behind. He slowly came over to her desk and said softly, "Miss Thompson…Miss Thompson, you smell just like my mother…and her bracelet looks real pretty on you, too. I'm glad you liked my presents.

The next day when the children came to school, they were welcomed by a new teacher. Miss Thompson had become a different person. She was no longer just a teacher, she was now a person committed to loving her children and doing things for them that would live on after her. She helped all the children, but especially the slow ones, and especially Teddy Stallard.

By the end of the school year, Teddy showed dramatic improvement. He had caught up with most of the students and was even ahead of some.

She didn't hear from Teddy for a long time. Then one day, she received a note that read:

Dear Miss Thompson,

I wanted you to be the first to know, I will be graduating second in my class.

Love,
Teddy Stallard

Four years later, another note came:

Dear Miss Thompson,

They just told me I will be graduating first in my class. I wanted you to be the first to know. The University has not been easy, but I liked it.

Love,
Teddy Stallard

And four years later:

Dear Miss Thompson,

As of today, I am Theodore Stallard, M.D. Isn't it amazing?! I wanted you to be the first to know. I am getting married next month, the 27th to be exact. I want you to come and sit where my mother would sit if she were alive. You are the only family I have now; Dad died last year.

> *Love,*
> *Teddy Stallard*

Miss Thompson went to that wedding and sat where Teddy's mother would have sat. She deserved to sit there; she had done something for Teddy that he could never forget. She was more than a teacher. She became Teddy Stallard's mentor.

Miss Thompson made a choice to live consciously. The principle of *use* played out in Teddy's life. It unlocked his potential in such a way that he became more than he would have ever dared to dream. It's a parallel principle, too, because you can't touch someone else without being touched yourself. How we truly view life and work serves to make up the assumptions with which we live and our view of others . . . and it shows. Taking the time to intentionally "see" beyond the bracelet and the perfume was a conscious choice. From that choice meaning was revealed.

Work becomes something far more than a way to earn a living, and life becomes an investment in others and in myself.

The principle of *use* is informative at multiple levels—one of which is the realization that each of us is uniquely fitted or gifted to do one thing well. The "one thing" idea is not so much a limiting statement as it is the recognition that we as human beings bear a uniqueness that places a spin on history never before present until our birth. Each of us is uniquely creative unlike any other. It logically follows that if we are the product of a Creator, then each human being is creative. The principle of *use* is about identifying and developing that core motivation within both others and ourselves to the benefit of humanity. And of course, it honors the Creator as well.

The PRINCIPLE
of RESPONSIBILITY

Once our "sweet spot" has been identified, and we are in the process of growing and developing our uniqueness, the principle of *responsibility* surfaces. It becomes apparent by necessity, in that, intrinsic to our individual uniqueness we have a mutual responsibility to one another. To whom much is given, much is required is not a statement of demand, but one of *responsibility* (See Luke, the Apostle, historian and medical doctor. Luke 12:48).

My uniqueness as a human being coupled with my view of life and work compels me to creatively seek to benefit my fellow man. If I know the solution to a haunting problem, or if I have the keys to unlock a door, or if I know the way of escape from a dangerous situation, I am by nature *responsible* to act. This then is the sense in which the principle of *responsibility* is stated. The uniqueness of each of us defines the "much given."

Denny, mentioned in the first chapter, is a farmer in Ohio and he works thousands of acres with very few people. His wise use of technology and informed botanical application has reduced the need for a labor-intensive business. However, several years ago a young man expressed significant interest and talent in agriculture, so Denny hired him to teach, train and develop a new generation. He didn't need the hired help, but he intentionally chose to build into the life of this young man. Denny is well past the proverbial retirement age, yet he refuses to quit.

Life is all about choices. We can choose to identify what it is we do well, turn it into a profitable vocation, amass a targeted amount of personal wealth and then retire to a beach, golf course or favorite fishing spot to sit, soak and sour until death does us part. That's a choice. It's a choice that reflects a view of life and work that I believe is inconsistent with the shape of reality.

Growing up in small town America in northeastern Kansas built a lot of good things into my life. Among them would be a good work ethic, valuing people and appreciating simple things. Work was a way of life. My grandfather, Jacob, worked to the day he died at age 90. Somewhere along the line the concept of "retirement" became fashionable. There seemed to be a not so gradual swing from enjoying a day of hard work to inventing escapisms from work. In some ways I don't think my grandfather worked a day in his life. As an old-fashioned farmer, he was in the fields from sunrise to sunset and loved it. In that sense, he never worked.

Fast forward to today and it's all about retiring. The radio DJ announces that it's Wednesday, tomorrow is Thursday, then comes the weekend to party; followed, of course, by the dreaded Monday. Work became something to endure, or make the best of, as we look forward to retirement, the ultimate weekend. Work has become simply a means to an end, a way to make a living. For my grandfather, work was his life. It was living. It included meaning, identity, creating and leaving a mark on history.

The logic in today's mindset escapes me. Our culture has deluded us. We grow up, receive a formal or informal education, apply our education in multiple ways throughout life, gain much wisdom from our mistakes and our successes . . .and then we "retire" (disengage). The media has lulled us into thinking that: (1) self-indulgence is wonderful and expected; (2) golfing the rest of our life is desirable; (3) living like a millionaire in a retirement community is the best life has to offer. I reject that. I'm all about slowing down a bit, doing some things one has not been able to do because circumstances and season of life have not allowed, but to disengage from life—NO. You and I have life experience, wisdom, understanding and skills the rest of the world sorely needs. Putting all that wisdom gained by life-experience out to pasture somewhere raises questions of morality. Besides that, truth be known, many of those so-called retired people are inwardly restless and struggle with their personal sense of meaning and significance. We are hardwired to be productive, to engage in life and to invest in others. Retire from your job, yes, but don't retire from living. Meaning and significance are derived from investing the uniqueness of who we are into the lives of others.

My intent in these comments is not to be unkind or dismissive of the choices one may make related to their concept of retirement. And by the way, I am not disparaging the sport of golf. I use it more as a metaphor. It is my intent, however, to cause us to at least push the pause button and think. The culture is making a statement and we may well be buying into something we did not intend. We live in a time when it is not at all uncommon for a person to be retired the same number of years he or she worked. Again, this principle of *responsibility* is directly tied to our assumptions about the value of life and work. Is work simply a way to pay the bills and get to a future date we can finally "do what we always wanted to do?"

I'm not so concerned that there are 10,000 people retiring each day as I am concerned about the meaning of the term, "retire." Retiring from something to begin something else is a good thing—but "disengagement" is not. Tragic to me is the prospect of thousands of uniquely gifted and wise human beings no longer taking the *responsibility* to engage life. A lifetime of work, experience and even mistakes adds up to a whole lot of wisdom from which the generation following us can benefit. And, we need to modify the definition of retiring.

I do believe there are some who struggle with the current idea of retiring, but they go with the flow anyway because it's what society expects. Retirement for one very financially well-off CEO now consists of floating around the ocean to various ports of call and catching fish. It is a wonderful and fun thing to do for a season of time—as a break from the usual—but it is not "a life" that has any meaning or fulfillment. Even a cursory observation of the principles of *use* and *responsibility* reveals a conflict in this kind of disengagement from life. It is our design as human beings to be productive and meaningfully engaged, for which there is no age limit.

Denny has an apartment in the country of Panama from which I am privileged to spend time writing. We take long walks together and talk. It intrigues me to listen and observe as he intuitively engages others. A young woman struggles to push a heavy wheel barrel over the curb. He moves to her side, smiles and takes the handles. He turns it around, pulling the wheel barrel backwards up and over the curb with ease. The light in her eyes reveals she gets it. I can imagine that every day she does the same thing and thinks of Denny, though she does not know him.

He talks about what he can do in Panama during the weeks he may be there. Perhaps he can befriend a Panamanian farmer and teach him to yield more corn on an acre from 50 to 100 to 200, even 300 bushels per acre. He's doing it in Ohio, why not here? It's a choice to engage when no one would blame him for simply doing nothing but relaxing. After all, he's earned it.

Don't misunderstand me here. He relaxes. He has fun. He enjoys life fully, AND he continually seeks ways to engage others.

The PRINCIPLE of FIDELITY

It was just a little thing but he was excited about his new job. Actually, it was his first job as a recent immigrant to the United States. He was a delivery truck driver for an American-based corporation called Seven-Eleven. He was emotionally upbeat and kind to everyone he met as he delivered from store to store. He had multiple stores on his regular route and everyone was always happy to see him because they were often encouraged by his kindness. He took it upon himself to make observations of needed changes about some of the little things that could make him more efficient in his job as a truck driver. It was his faithfulness to the little things of his job that made him so unusual; a principle called *fidelity*.

It happened that a new hire was assigned to ride with him for one week to be trained in the various aspects of the Seven-Eleven enterprise. He eagerly accepted his new role as trainer and informed this trainee of all his daily duties. He also talked of his dreams. As an immigrant, one day he wanted to have his own Seven-Eleven store. Every day for one week the trainee observed the delivery truck driver, his impact on people and his attention to detail. When the training period ended, he expressed his appreciation for the training and for the trainer's attitude. The trainee had learned much.

Time passed and one day the truck driver was called to the home office of Seven-Eleven for a meeting. He was not clear as to the purpose of the meeting; it was just a meeting. The invitation to the home office seemed strange, but of course he went. He sat in the waiting room along with various other employees of Seven-Eleven from all over the country who had also been called. His turn came to go into the office of the CEO, and sitting behind the desk was his "trainee" who rode with him for a week—the CEO of Seven-Eleven. The company is so big only a few know the CEO by sight, so the CEO took positive advantage of that and sometimes posed as a regular employee—just to see what really happens day to day in his stores and to observe the employees' attitudes as well as hear their comments regarding other fellow employees. The CEO desired to be helpful and encouraging to his employees, always striving to make Seven-Eleven a better place. He was very pleased by this delivery truck driver's proactive attention to his job. The CEO told him he wasn't going to be driving a delivery truck anymore. He was getting his own store. It began as a little thing, and it grew into a big thing.

An inseparable component to *fidelity* is trust. The driver demonstrated his trustworthiness with the proverbial little things of his job. If you can be trusted with a truck and all the related unseen things of the job, then being trusted with a high profile store is a no brainer. Why? Trust is trust. That doesn't change.

Actually the use of the terms "little things" and "big things" is largely a play on words to make a point. In reality, the little things ARE the big things. There are no little things. The driver never saw his work as a little thing. His whole approach to work, including his attitude and dependability, demonstrated this principle of *fidelity*. Beware of the tendency to measure job value by significance. It may tell you more than you want to know about yourself. The principles don't change with the job.

A young man graduated from the university with a degree in Finance. He always dreamed of working toward being a CFO one day. He was hired by a large electrical organization, active in nearly every state in the USA. Every morning at 5:00 he was up and out the door to the construction site, rain or shine, cold or hot. For months he climbed around inside a huge building learning about the electrical wiring. He was a construction worker. He was learning a trade. He was diligent—day-to-day—without complaint.

The owner and CEO called him in to the office one day. He was informed that yesterday was his last day on the construction site. Now he would be doing a variety of things around the office, still learning, still diligent. Along the way the CEO provided the time and finances for him to earn his MBA. Today, six years later, he is the company Controller, taking on more and more responsibility and his story continues.

Barbara loves her work in sales at the women's clothing store. She engages her customers with enthusiasm and personal interest always seeking to serve her customers' needs. This particular store prides itself in customer satisfaction and empowers each employee to use their own judgment in meeting customers' needs.

She had a long time customer looking for a particular size and color of a dress. The store had the size but not the color. Time was an issue for the shopper as she needed the dress for an upcoming event. The lady left the store a little disappointed. Later that day a shipment was received for the store and in it was the color dress she needed. Barbara called her and told the happy lady her dress was in. Barbara told her I will bring it to you when I get off work. She drove sixty miles to deliver the dress to her customer.

Barbara was not asked to do this; she took it upon herself to do so. This is another example of fidelity in the workplace. In one sense it's a little thing; it is being very faithful and attentive to a customer's need and making a creative decision to meet it. No doubt the store also secured the business of a good customer.

There are a lot of things at play in this narrative beyond the principle of fidelity, and that is always the case. "Reciprocity" and "use" are readily identifiable. The store not only showed wisdom in identifying an excellent sales person, but the store also put a lot of thought and emphasis on training and development of their staff. They successfully created a positive business culture that released Barbara to be creatively unique.

Dave is the General Manager of a restaurant my wife and I frequent. We have become friends and now we feel very much a part of the 'restaurant family'. Dave always wanted to be a coach. He loves sports and volunteers his time with various community sports opportunities.

He has that "coaches attitude" about him. Over time I have watched him engage his wait staff, managers, cooks, greeters and those who bus the tables. One day in conversation I looked at Dave and said, "Dave, you ARE a coach." He smiled and then laughed and said, "Yes, I know."

As is the case with many restaurants, it is a transition job for most. His young staff is often working there to earn money for college and in some cases simply to supplement the family income. Of course, there are the career people but for the most part they are there only long enough to transition to something else.

Dave sees his staff as fifty individually unique people. He takes the time to discover their gifts, dreams, ever changing life themes, struggles, needs, and so on. They are not there simply to serve the needs of the company, but they are human beings "on his team" for a time and he has the opportunity to build, develop, encourage and grow them to a better place before they move on. It takes time, effort and concern for something greater than the profit motive; however, the culture created in the restaurant translates to a very profitable enterprise.

He is very engaged in the 'little things' of his staff's lives. When they walk in the door for their shift he greets them uniquely because he knows where they are coming from. Some need a hug, others a word of encouragement or just simply that someone notices them. He recalls former conversations and picks up on a subject of concern or a recent life accomplishment like a good grade on a test. One of his wait staff left for a "better opportunity" somewhere, and Dave told him the door is always open. He was gone for a time and came back. Dave told me when he left he would be back. "They need to know they can come home," he said.

Dave 'builds' into their lives, and he does it with intentionality. Yes, he has a store to run and desires it to be profitable, and it is. Even though it is a transition job for many as I mentioned, many slow that transition because it has become more than a place to earn money. It has in many ways become a 'team'. Some did not know what they were good at until they came and the 'coach' helped them discover and develop it.

It's interesting to me that even when people have days off they choose to come to the restaurant where they work, to eat and hang out. Others who have moved on and are developing in their career path make it their restaurant of choice when going out to dinner. Dave is the General Manager, but more than that, he is really a 'life coach'. The sum total of years of the 'little things' faithfully and consciously executed continue to be wonderfully rewarding, both personally and professionally.

Fidelity is a choice, however. And the inclination to make the choice is indicative of a healthy view of life and work. Life has intrinsic value and work is a way of expressing our uniqueness as a human being. Remember The Cultural Mandate concept that was discussed earlier? Our original purpose as human beings was to create cultures and build civilizations.

These principles are a choice in that they don't come naturally. However, we as human beings find ourselves resonating well when we personally experience treatment that is characterized by these eight principles. At first glance, this may appear a contradiction, but closer scrutiny informs us otherwise. There is no contradiction between choice and consequence.

The PRINCIPLE of GREATNESS

Great people serve people; a counter intuitive principle, to be sure. Following a seminar in Kiev, Ukraine I was standing to the side of the meeting room in discussion with the CEO, CFO and COO of a large restaurant chain headquartered in Kiev. They clearly enjoyed and appreciated the seminar on Servant Leadership, presented by the Chick-fil-A team of seven. Nearly all the Ukrainian participants were gone, so several of our team members were busy cleaning up the empty water bottles and other debris left by our fifty attendees.

As we talked I noticed that Marina, the young COO of the company, broke eye contact with me and looked around the room. She was watching one of the Chick-fil-A team members busily gathering waste and straightening the area. With tears in her eyes, she commented, "He IS a servant." At dinner that evening I told the team about the incident. The few minutes of modeling servant leadership demonstrated the entire two-day seminar in a nutshell for Marina. Talking the talk is easy; walking the walk is a choice. The tears in her eyes reflected the resonance with her life. She lives in a culture where the boss is typically the one who gets served.

However, no matter what the culture, there is a tendency in all of us who find ourselves in a place of leadership to *expect* to be served. *Greatness* serves others. The president of the company is there to serve his people in a manner that will make them successful. Knowing Chick-fil-A as I do, this incident with Marina was not surprising. The CEO of Chick-fil-A serves his people daily in the practical "little things" of life. I hear stories of him walking an employee to the car on a rainy day, holding an umbrella to keep them dry. That's *greatness* . . . and it's contagious.

In the previous story of the Seven-Eleven CEO, it is apparent that serving his people is a major motivation in his life. He stepped out of his comfort zone and did something no one would have expected, nor would anyone have blamed him if he had remained in the comfort of his office. Truly *great* people serve people. The question we should ask ourselves daily is, "What does serving look like in my sphere of influence?" Sometimes it takes some creative, out of the box thinking, but it's fun!

A friend of mine served for many years as the CEO of a large engineering firm in Dallas, Texas. I recall the first time I visited Gary in his office building. Of course I expected to be ushered into a large and plush corner office—after all, he's the CEO. Instead, he greeted me at the entrance of the building and walked me around to meet his colleagues. The room was a very large open area filled with cubicles. His cubicle was in the center of the room, no larger or smaller than anyone else's. The positive reputation of the firm's culture told the story.

This kind of leadership is a choice to resist what people expect a CEO to do. This is the kind of *greatness* that causes all of us to happily and eagerly want to follow.

Greatness is not to be confused with a "position."

Greatness is a principle of life one chooses to exercise—no matter his station. Making that choice is, however, often more difficult for one who achieves a higher level of notoriety or fame in their field. It is partly because they think they deserve it, and it is partly due to societal expectation. It's not really a matter of right or wrong, either. It is more a wisdom choice than it is anything else.

I recall an occasion some years ago when I was in search of a new car. I was pointed to a particular dealership in the area. They had a reputation for fairness from just about everyone I encountered. I was told the name of the owner and was encouraged to ask for him. The dealership bore his name, and when I asked for Eddie they motioned me to the large shop area. It was filled with cars being serviced, and out from under each car protruded a pair of legs! I kept asking for Eddie and was finally pointed to a particular vehicle. I spoke to the pair of legs sticking out from under the car, again asking for Eddie. Out came Eddie, greasy hands and all, with a big smile on his face. Someone else could run the store; he loved being under the cars out back with his men. They loved it too. That service area was the heart of his business and it was his heart, too. I bought a car from Eddie. *Greatness* is a choice . . . and sometimes it's a choice to resist the expectations of others and our culture.

John and Jean have been real estate agents for years. They want the customer to have the home that is best for their family, not the home that generates the most commission. They even talk customers out of certain purchases, knowing it's not good for them in the long term. I've seen them coach people to buy less costly homes for the sake and well-being of the customer. They have gone without their commission, on occasion, to benefit their customer. It is not unusual for a closing on a home to cost them something personally because in their eyes "it is best" for the buyer. They throw an annual party in a local hotel for their past clients. It rivals all the amenities of a large wedding reception—

complete with DJ, food, dancing and prizes. *Greatness* comes in all sizes and shapes. They would never frame themselves as *great*, but *greatness* looks for ways to serve people . . . and they do.

The appointment ended, we said our goodbyes and I quickly exited the coffee shop. During my drive home I realized I left my blue tooth ear piece on the tray. I went back and asked the young man clearing the tables if he saw the ear piece. He had not. After a brief look around and peering into the trash container of food waste and paper, I left. It was too much to ask anyone to search through all that garbage, and besides, it was my own fault.

Several days later I was back in the same coffee shop for an appointment. Out of curiosity I asked the young lady who took my order if they happened to have found an ear piece. I fully expected the answer to be, "No." But since I was there I thought I would just ask. She smiled, picked up an ear piece from beside the cash register and said, "This one?" It was the one. She told me that after hearing of my lost ear piece the young man who cleared the table quickly took the trash can out back and carefully picked through the entire thing. That is *greatness*. He made a choice to serve a customer whom he did not know. *Great* people serve people whether they are a CEO or the one who cleans up after everyone has eaten. It's not a matter of position; it's a matter of choice.

Now we can begin to see the interplay of these principles. The young man busing tables exercised *reciprocity, fidelity* and *greatness* with a strong touch of *responsibility*.

Where one principle is discovered the others are not far away.

The PRINCIPLE of PERSEVERANCE

Each of us is captured by a story of *perseverance*, and the corresponding success that comes to the one who does not quit. Movies revel in it, history is written by it and life today would be very different without it. Our hearts are warmed and challenged by the motion picture stories of *Secretariat*, *Gladiator*, William Wallace in *Braveheart* and the passions of others who refused to quit. The sports world is filled with accounts of athletes who prevailed against seemingly impossible odds when quitting would have been both expected and accepted.

As a young man, Walter was fired from his newspaper job because he lacked creativity. He wanted to be a commercial artist and was not defeated by this early rejection. His first business failed, leaving him so financially destitute he resorted to eating dog food. As early as he could remember he was always a doodler and drawer. He created a little rabbit character which had some promise—only to learn later that the idea was stolen and secretly patented by someone else. Again, down but not out, he forged ahead. He developed a crude mouse character that was rejected because it was thought to scare women. The world is a better place because Walt Disney never quit.

Pamela Travers, born in Australia, was living in England at the time she wrote a novel called *Mary Poppins* which was published in 1934. Walt Disney's daughter, Diane, loved the book which alerted her father to the idea of considering it for a movie. He went to England in 1945 to ask her for the rights to make the novel into a screenplay for making a movie. She refused and kept refusing for the next fourteen years—

in spite of his relentless attention, flattery and inter-continental telegrams. Because she finally succumbed to his charm and persistence—nineteen years' worth of *perseverance*—the world has a timeless classic in the movie, *Mary Poppins*, which premiered on August 27, 1964.

We enjoy Hershey chocolate today because a man name Milton Hershey never quit. Ultimately, he earned the title, "the chocolate king." That's how the story ends, but the story itself contains a timeless message. At age fourteen he dropped out of school with an interest in candy making, and he apprenticed himself to a master confectioner. After four years of study and experience, he borrowed $150 from his aunt and began his own business. He worked long hard hours for five years— only to find success to be elusive. His business failed but his entrepreneurial drive did not. He moved to Denver, discovered caramel and how to use milk to make it. Two more business ventures failed—one in Chicago and the other in New York City.

He went back to his home of Lancaster, Pennsyl-vania and started what became known as the very successful Lancaster Caramel Company. In 1893 he attended a business exposition in Chicago and became fascinated with art of making chocolate. He was especially interested in using milk to make chocolate, which up to this time in history was pretty much the domain of the Swiss. He developed a formula which allowed him to mass produce and mass distribute milk chocolate.

In 1900 he sold his caramel company and focused entirely on chocolate, quickly surpassing the success of his former company many times over. He had a vision to make chocolate readily available to the masses, and he did. The world continues to enjoy the many expressions of his *perseverance* via brands that include Almond Joy, Mounds, Cadbury, Reese's, Twizzlers and Hershey Kisses. In addition, Pennsylvania has a model community called Hershey. He established a school for children that operates to this day, and via the Hershey Foundation continues to fund educational and cultural activities internationally.

It occurs to me that the world would be missing a lot but for the *perseverance* of some. Of course, if there was no Disney Corporation with all the attending benefits to the public, the public would never know. But we do know and it is difficult for us to imagine a world without Disney, or perhaps chocolate without Hershey. It gives me pause to wonder what the world may miss if I quit, or if you quit. Could it be that just around the next corner, beyond the next failure, there is something grand to experience and to share? What is NOT a part of our experience today because someone failed a few times and got discouraged and decided to give up? We will never know, but I can only imagine that there is something we are missing . . . because some do quit.

I've mentioned the higher profile, even somewhat glamorous stories, to display the principle of *perseverance*. However, they are no less meaningful. Every walk of life has its stories. Consider the stories of *perseverance* that are more "ordinary," yet nonetheless important. Think about the man or woman who lives faithfully and consistently in their daily life, raises a family, provides love and shelter to their children and launches them into life as productive citizens. Or picture the young man who works to overcome the dysfunction of his own childhood and struggles as a husband and father to provide the masculine guidance needed for his role. Imagine the young lady who struggles her entire life with intimacy due to a sexual abuse experience in her early life. Or reflect on the single mom who never gets a break and finally sees her child reach adulthood . . . and maybe have some of the things she never had.

These are stories of *perseverance* we'll never read about on the Internet or in a book. Most of us will not even hear about them. Nevertheless, those stories are just as real and determinative. It may not result in multiple theme parks being built around the world for all to enjoy, but it does introduce into society another healthy functioning adult who will go on to benefit those whom they touch. It does make the world a better place and honors the Creator. It writes another story in the history of the world.

Perseverance, too, is a choice. It is a daily choice, to keep on keeping on. Therein lays the difficulty of it. Anyone can make a healthy choice "once." But making that same choice day after day after day is the difficult part. Perhaps part of it is the ability to see failure and difficulty as part of a process rather than as a destination. That, too, is a choice.

There is an ancient story, over 4000 years old, of a young teenage boy taken captive by slave traders and taken to Egypt during the time of the Pharaohs. He was sold to an Egyptian leader named Potiphar, who had many slaves.

It was a serious sibling rivalry that created the situation that resulted in his being taken captive. Joseph was from a large family typical of that time. He was next to the youngest of twelve brothers and an unknown number of sisters. His brothers were jealous of him for the attention paid him by their father. They conspired to teach him a lesson by throwing him into a dry water cistern in the desert and leaving him there. When a slave caravan came by the area, some of the brothers had the idea of selling him to them and then telling their father that a wild animal had killed him. That's how Joseph ended up in Egypt.

Rejected by his own brothers and now believed dead by the rest of the family, Joseph is alone in a foreign culture. No one would have blamed Joseph for using his circumstances as an excuse to quit. However, he did not.

Potiphar quickly identified something in Joseph worth investing in and put Joseph in charge of his household, overseeing the other slaves. Potiphar traveled a lot in his job and was absent for long periods of time, which placed even greater trust in and responsibility on Joseph. Potiphar's wife tried unsuccessfully on multiple occasions to seduce Joseph. Finally, in a fit of frustration and anger at his rejection of her advances, she framed him for rape. Potiphar returned from his trip, learned of the situation and put Joseph in prison where he remained for some years. Still another set of unfair circumstances, but Joseph chose not to quit. Soon the head jailer observed similar qualities in Joseph as Potiphar had apparently seen. The jailer put Joseph in charge of the prisoners.

Through a series of circumstances, Joseph helped a fellow prisoner get an early release. When he returned to his former job, Joseph asked the newly released prisoner to mention his name in various conversations in hopes that people would remember Joseph, and maybe he could get out of prison, too. But, the fellow prisoner forgot to mention Joseph's name to anyone. "No good deed goes unpunished" is an often-heard comment. I can imagine Joseph must of thought of that saying often! He helped a fellow inmate get a legitimate release and then when things were going well for him in his job serving the Pharaoh, that inmate forgot all about Joseph. Remarkably, Joseph never quit.

One day through a series of unusual circumstances, Joseph was able to assist the Pharaoh with a very perplexing personal problem related to a dream he had. The Pharaoh was so pleased he released Joseph and brought him into the palace, making him what amounts to the Prime Minister of Egypt. No one was greater in Egypt than Joseph, except Pharaoh. Some years later that entire part of the world experienced a devastating famine. Due to Joseph's wisdom and leadership, many lives were spared.

Easily identified in this story is *perseverance*. Joseph never quit. In addition, he demonstrated other principles that we've already observed—*reciprocity*, *responsibility*, *fidelity* and *greatness*. Notice how these principles function. They are all working in concert with one another.

The PRINCIPLE of CHANGE

Also operative in this ancient story is the principle of *change*. Changing direction without changing his principles was a continual challenge. We see it in Joseph finding himself in the bottom of the pit; then again as a slave and as a falsely-accused prisoner, and finally as Prime Minister of Egypt. Circumstances changed constantly but who he was on the inside remained the same. His consistency of character showed in his decision-making, attitudes and behavior. I am not suggesting this was easy for Joseph. I can only imagine he had his down times when it must have been difficult to keep going. Knowing the end of the story, we are aware he did not use his dysfunctional family of origin as an excuse; nor did he give up and become a part of the system of betrayal and unfairness in which he found himself.

Each of us is intuitively aware that change is a part of life. Some changes are big ones, life altering perhaps. Pamela Travers' father died when she was seven, and Milton Hershey was ten when his father was no longer a part of the family picture. What we do with the change makes all the difference. How we personally manage the pain of it and choose to channel the attending emotion is telling. All of us are on the inside of ourselves looking out. That adds a subjectivity to change that makes managing it that much more difficult and sensitive.

Bahar works for a large international conglomerate in the financial services division located in a small Central Asian country. She has excelled within the company and loves working with her American manager. She would often comment with great pleasure on the management style of her immediate supervisor. It stood in stark contrast to what she was accustomed to culturally.   Her comments always related to the manner in which she was treated. The climate of her work situation was such that she looked forward to going to the office. It was not unusual for her to willingly stay longer hours to complete a task for a desired deadline. She was always treated respectfully and appropriately praised when a job was well done. She was so happy to work for an American company rather than a local company whose business culture was far less accommodating.

One day her immediate director announced his transfer to a neighboring country, and he was replaced by one of her own countrymen. Her supervisor was now one from her own culture and everything changed. The negative cultural stigma for her being younger, single and female surfaced quickly. Work became unpleasant. Projects were piled on her with unfair expectations in the hopes she would grow weary and quit. Working longer hours was now expected to complete the added tasks. She received no verbal appreciation or thanks. Attempts to disparage her achievements were frequent. There was a sense in which she always had to watch her back. Even as I write, the story continues. She remains in this seemingly cultural trap caught between the reality of working in an American company but relating to a male superior who carries a cultural bias that puts her in a difficult spot. Her job did not change, but the reporting relationship and office culture significantly changed for the worse. We have spent hours discussing her situation. I am impressed with her resolve to remain consistent, productive and positive as an employee. She bears up well under the unfair treatment and the attempts to discredit her work. She told me she will not change her principles because "this is who I am." She will continue to be who she is in her heart and try not to allow the circumstances to dissuade her. Hearing the details of many of her stories made her choice even that much more meaningful to me. Little do they know how good of an employee they have. Many would simply give up—making a "victim of circumstance" claim to justify whatever choice is made. The emotional toll on her is obvious. When we parted company, she smiled and said, "This will make me stronger."

I boarded my plane for the long journey back to the States saddened that she was rather trapped in the peculiarities of her culture's attitudes toward women. Shortly after arriving back home, however, I received a joy filled email from her informing me she was going to France to study for a second Master's diploma then on to a Phd. Her experience is an example of 'change' on Steroids. Thirty years old and so much is a "first" for her including living on her own, making her own choices, staying out as late as she wishes, choosing her friends, spending her own money, choosing a field of study, having a living space she shares with no one and the list grows daily. She informed me she would often awaken in the middle of the night crying because she never before knew the feeling of freedom. How she has managed the change continues to be quite remarkable.

In October 1965, The Byrds, a folk-based band from Los Angeles released what became an internationally best selling hit, Turn-Turn-Turn (to Everything There is a Season). The song was based entirely on an Old Testament passage (Chapter 3:1) in a book called

Ecclesiastes. This 3000 year old document both records and laments the idea of 'change'. It continues to resonate with us today because the theme of change is something we all intuitively identify with, each for our own reasons and in our own ways.

A friend of mine, Kurt, commented in a conversation we were having about 'change' that we usually associate it with discomfort. That's an excellent point. His thought was to reframe the concept a bit. The aforementioned ancient document uses the concept of "season". Intellectually, we are all aware of the changing seasons, no matter where we live. Most often the change is not all that noticeable, but the change is happening nevertheless. From time to time we are made abruptly aware of the change, but for the most part it is subtle and gradual. There is a kind of intuitive awareness and acceptance of this change. This creates an environment of expectancy which allows us to participate in change rather than seek to control it. This is not to be confused with fatalism; actually just the opposite is true. Participating, managing and engaging change as an involved player allows no room for fatalism.

When I met Kurt he was one of the vice presidents of a very large company, in charge of the mattress division. It was a very comfortable and rewarding position in a company that was a "household word" in his niche area. Kurt places a high value on open and honest communication in life in general and the workplace in particular. This was very important to him within the team of six with whom he worked. This was a place he could spend the remainder of his working career. However, he began to see open and honest communication deteriorate from higher up in the company. It came down to him in the form of a directive to begin to let some key people in his area of affairs go and to do so just weeks before the Christmas holiday. This was anything but 'honest or open'. This directive very much violated the core character of who Kurt is. Kurt resigned and left the company not knowing his next steps. As we talked about this he realizes had it not been for this unwanted change, he never would have left his job and never would have been moved to do the things he did. It was interesting and curious to him that 'change' was needed in one area to initiate 'change' in another. His reputation as a open and honest business man generated a following that very naturally carried Kurt into a successful four year period of consulting work. He was sought out by others for his wisdom and experience because they trusted his character. It was during this four year adventure in consulting he resurfaced an old idea that had been cooking within him for some time. He wanted to make and sell a Latex mattress. He rolled out and developed the idea into reality. A couple of years into his new company development he was acquired by the company from whom he had been purchasing his latex material. There are a lot more details as you can imagine, but suffice it to say, had it not been for the 'change' occurring all around him necessitating he make changes, there would never have been any 'changes'. That's why Kurt said that we often view change as uncomfortable. In reality, in his case, 'change' dislodged Kurt from a very comfortable place to a far better place. He managed his change well, rather than seek to control it in some manner. Kurt said that for him part of his 'change' was to stop doing what he was not good at and focus on what he is good at. Again, this is often something we fail to do until 'change' makes it necessary. He said that since 'change' is constantly moving, the choice we have is whether we are to move forward or backwards. He chose forward. He's in a good place right now; things are comfortable and the future looks profitable and bright. However, he is keenly aware, "for everything there is a season". Change is happening......always.

Change is a constant in life. Circumstances don't make us—they reveal us. What's on the inside is going to reveal itself sooner or later. Wisdom informs us to thoughtfully consider the inner choices of character. Change is wise when circumstances necessitate it. Life and work is filled with change. It's a simple concept and profoundly significant when one considers the character implications.

The PRINCIPLE of UNITY

There is a very old proverb that states, "A house divided cannot stand". Whether in our home, organization, company or as an individual, there is a necessity for coherence within the system. The principle of unity is a by-product of a life lived truthfully. Ideas, concepts, beliefs and values matter, and it matters that there is an agreement/resonance within my life experiences. To the extent this is true—to that same extent unity is experienced. A culture is created within an organization that is positive, caring and productive. When these eight principles are operative, there is a corresponding positive consequence. The ancients were correct in their observations. Unity cannot be dictated, mandated or manipulated. Where there is a spirit of unity, one will also discover that people are engaged in meaningful work. The two are inseparable; when meaning is diminished, so too is unity diminished.

An excellent example of a unified positive company culture that I have observed is the Chick-fil-A Corporation, located in Atlanta, Georgia. Ten plus years of association with them, via scores of people who work in the company, has profoundly confirmed the on-going presence of these principles within the company's culture. Ask almost any customer and their feedback will not be so much about their excellent food as it is about their excellence as a company. Eating at one of their restaurants makes people feel like they are contributing to something good—in addition to getting a tasty meal and a great value. Also, their hiring process reveals the presence of a view of life and work that permeates the organization. Chemistry, character and competence are three of the things they look for in a new employee and in that order, as well. The first two are not "trainable." Even this makes a strong statement about the company and their priorities. It shows in all kinds of ways—including the extremely low turnover rate of both full-time and part-time employees. They lead the industry in their extraordinarily high retention rates. This is yet another positive consequence of an environment of unity. People like to stay connected when and where they find it.

Principles by definition tend to be static. That doesn't make them less real or in any way diminish their validity. It's just that until practiced, they make little to no difference. 'Unity' happens as a result of the choice to practice the principles. The whole point of the many stories and illustrations is to demonstrate 'practice' whether individually or corporately. They, also, demonstrate how we may choose to practice a principle is very unique to each of us. Practicing a principle both validates it and gives it life; otherwise, they are empty words. Each of us knows and understands the disillusionment of the proliferation of empty words.

Unity is something we sense. We are most aware of it when it is absent. It is an environment created when the contributing factors are in place and operative. It characterizes businesses, families, groups, clubs, associations and not to be overlooked, the individual. I was having breakfast with a friend, Emery, discussing this whole matter and he reminded me that if there is not a unity within the person, it will not flow to the larger environment. You cannot impart what you do not possess. He commented that when he was in his early thirties he was made aware of the necessity of defining his personal core values. It's not like he didn't have values, he just had never sat down and put them into words on a piece of paper. It was a lot more difficult than he thought it would be. Now, nearly three decades and multiple employment and business situations later, the unifying influence in his life continue to be the core values/principles he identified. "My values allow me to say 'no' to good things that come my way. In my years with commercial real estate I have been offered some very attractive and good opportunities to which I said, no, because they did not fit my values." He further stated that his nature is to stay nested and comfortable. However, he knows better because the lessons he has learned along the way have always followed his choices and his choices have been deeply rooted in his core values. "What people will say about me at my funeral matters to me." There is an undeniable unity in his life of choice making. As we talked, he was in the middle of yet another life transition which was taking him back to his original vision included in which are his core values. Unity isn't just a corporate thing, it's very personal, as well.

MEANING has a SHAPE

This whole discussion goes to the premise of how human beings are "wired." Another way of describing it is the idea of "design." By nature, human beings resonate with principles reflective of the shape of reality. Treating people in a manner we ourselves wish to be treated is a universal principle. In that sense, it resonates with the way we human beings are hardwired. The Eight Principles are reflective of that "shape." Foundational to these principles is the view of life I have, along with the value I place on work (as per the earlier discussion from Nancy Pearcey's book, the Cultural Mandate in Genesis 1:28 informs us that Creation was created "very good," implicit in which is humanity's task of both building culture and harnessing nature, a mandate never rescinded.)

Some of this may have become covered over in time with the vicissitudes of life, but it is this author's conviction that latent within us is the design.

There is a wonderful story of a Sea Lion in John Eldredge's book, *The Journey of Desire*. For my purposes I will call it "The Parable of the Sea Lion." In the story he captures the struggle between restlessness and complacency. The Sea Lion senses he is made (hardwired) for the sea, yet at the same time he has wandered far from it. He has forgotten who he is and for what he is made. His experience of the desert has covered his awareness of what he is. Somewhere along the way something within him is triggered and awakened. It is a long story so I will summarize it in the following manner.

Once upon a time there was a Sea Lion
who lost the sea. He lived in a barren desert

like wasteland. His daily experience was spent on a rock next to a very small and dirty body of water, surrounded by sand. At night he would look up at the stars and often dream strange dreams of being surrounded by water. His only companion was a tortoise. He would tell his strange dreams to the tortoise who would in turn tell him to forget his dreamy ideas and make the best of his current situation. Yet, he continued to dream. He could not help himself. It was as if something within him beckoned him, to what, he did not know for sure. The tortoise kept telling the Sea Lion that this little bit of water was fine. He could splash about in it as much as he wished. However, the Sea Lion knew there was something more. His dreams were of a great expanse of water the ends of which were seemingly limitless. The tortoise became frustrated with the Sea Lion's endless dreams. I have a secret to tell you, said the tortoise. I am not a tortoise, at all. I am a sea turtle. A long time ago I purposely left the sea

> *in search of something better. He told the Sea Lion wonderful tales of the sea which seemed to sooth the Sea Lion for a time. Then one day the Sea Lion slipped from his rock and began moving toward the east. The tortoise, surprised, asked where he was going? "I am off to find the sea", said the Sea Lion with great confidence and determination.*

The principles are not magic; they are life principles. They reflect a life truthfully lived. A consequence of a life truthfully lived is a life lived in concert with the shape of reality. Yet again, it reflects our wiring. There is a sidebar to the story of the Sea Lion worth noting and it concerns the Tortoise. He was aware of his origins but for unknown reasons ignored or rejected it. He chose to remain in the complacency of his desert. Doing so greatly diminished his life experience. However, operate anything according to the manufacturer's specifications and you'll find that it works better. That's the point. Life and work have a definitive shape and these principles are representative of the shape of reality.

Remember my friend, Denny— the one who works and plays hard? Is he retired? No. He told me he's not going to retire either. "What? Leave all this fun? Why would I do that?" That's Denny and that's his choice. Does he relax? Yes. I'm sitting in his warm weather apartment now on the 47th floor overlooking the ocean. He plays basketball at night here in Panama with young men a third his age who complain because he plays too hard. Playing is not something Denny does to get away from work. He loves both his work and his play. I am not suggesting we model our lives after Denny and do the same. I am suggesting we consider life and work and our view of it. It makes all the difference.

Do what you love and you will never work a day in your life. In some cases that is going to mean making a choice to view life and work according to the shape of reality. So much of life is about choices and choices have consequences both by commission and omission. Lead your life; don't let it lead you.

I met him at a Christmas dinner party at the home of a mutual friend. Early in the conversation I learned he had somewhat recently retired from his lifelong work at an international company. He and his wife purchased a recreational vehicle and were traveling the United States, golfing. He proudly commented he had golfed 200 days that year. Golfing a lot was something he always wanted to do, and I must say it was nice to hear it was something he and his wife could share. However, I couldn't help but think about the idea of engaging life. It's not a judgment statement so much as it is a question of wondering how long he will find it satisfying. I can see taking a season of life and doing something one has always wanted to do, but making it your entire life is another thing. Our hard wiring doesn't shut down at a certain age. What it looks like will change, of course, but the core motivation does not. Each of us is uniquely created. We find our sense of meaning in expressing that uniqueness and there is no expiration date.

Truett Cathy, at age 90, still goes to the office regularly. Why? The cynic may say it's because he's a workaholic, control freak, bored, hands on, etc. But those who know Truett will tell you it's because he loves it. He loves being engaged. In his own words he will tell you that Chick-fil-A is not about chicken—it's about people. If it were about chicken he would have stopped coming into the office a long time ago.

Ask yourself what your work is about. If there is an unrest about your employment it may not be because you have the wrong job; it may be your perspective about the job. Perspective is huge. However, both the job and your perspective can be changed. If work is something you do with an attitude that thinks, "I can't wait to get away from here every weekend" or "I can't wait for thirty years to be over so I can leave this place," then you've got a real problem. Sadly, if that's your thought pattern you will waste those thirty years— tolerating rather than engaging life.

A person who truly engages life doesn't view work as something to get away from. They view it as their tool of choice at that time in their life to engage life. The tools will change but the engagement need not. So called "retirement" does not necessarily mean disengaging from life. However, our culture pushes us hard to move in that direction. Sadly, they often become one and the same. Just listen to the comments and jokes the next time you're at a retirement party. It tells the story.

I was in Jamaica attending a seminar. I recall a group of gentlemen well into their seventies and early eighties who banded together for a common cause to engage in some specific humanitarian activities. The spokesperson for the group was explaining their activity and said, "No matter how old you get, you never lose that need to be significantly engaged." Again, it's about our hard wiring. It's also about "'choice" to align ourselves with it.

MAKING the CHOICE to ENGAGE

Darrell and Pat are in their eighties as I write this; but then I am getting ahead of myself. In 1997 they were in Svetlovodsk, Ukraine working as volunteers with the local educational system. They observed a city filled with so much need they decided to do something. They started a mission to feed the hungry, provide clothing and supply medicines to the extent they could. Pat was a psychiatric nurse and Darrell had been an electrical engineer in Pennsylvania. They decided to fund their mission primarily with their retirement income, and to this day they are still involved and still funding it—

yet physically unable to visit the mission. At first it was just the two of them engaging the people of Svetlovodsk. And then others at home in the U.S.A. heard of their vision and got involved with them.

In my occasional phone conversations with Pat, she speaks with great passion of her friends in Ukraine, the mission and the fun of seeing it become almost entirely self-funded. Due to declining health Darrell lives life relatively unaware of his surroundings, yet Pat continues on with what is still their combined vision. No one would have faulted them if they had retired to a comfortable life—earned by their years of professional work. It was expected. But they chose to do the unexpected and the unusual. They found a dream, engaged it with the resources they had and watched the dream blossom to the extent it became the dream of others. Of course, in Svetlovodsk there are thousands whose lives have been significantly impacted over the years by Darrell and Pat's choice to engage.

Each of us has within our beings a desire to engage; to make a difference. Culture sometimes places upon us an expectation contrary to what we both feel and know to do, and that's where the need for "choice" emerges. Sometimes we need to choose against the cultural expectations of our age and follow the Creator-the One who placed that hard wiring within our deepest parts. What that looks like for each of us is unique. Perhaps we need to set our faces to "finding the Sea."

My wife and I have some friends that are always posting what's going on in their lives on Facebook. The interesting thing about Ken and Grace is that they are nearly seventy and "retired"—but they are not disengaged. That's the point of all the Facebook postings. They are always out and about and doing something that would broadly fall into community and public service.

They both volunteer at summer youth camps, doing just about anything they can. Ken is called "Mr. Music" as he shares his gift of music wherever it is requested. When they are not doing summer camps, they stay busy visiting people who can't leave their homes due to mobility issues. Their activity is admirable, but even more noble is their choice to engage.

Each of us has something in common. We have a lifetime of experiences, training, skills and relationships. The "wisdom bank" we have made deposits into over the years is now equipped to make deposits into the lives of others. It doesn't even make business sense to take a lifetime investment and disengage. The opposite of self-indulgence is to engage.

There are a many things in life that "say easy" but "do hard." The business of engaging life meaningfully is at the top of that list, for it requires a conscious act of continuous choice-making. The Tortoise didn't want to make the effort and settled for a desert experience.

Rick is in his early 40s. He attended a well-known undergraduate university and a world-renowned business school. Through a set of circumstances (not of his own making), as well as a personal family tragedy, he is millions of dollars in debt. Many have encouraged him to just declare bankruptcy and move on. However, creditors and vendors to whom he owes money are his first priority. There are cases where he cannot pay all of his debt, but at least he is paying something on the dollar. He is far from being out of the proverbial woods, but in my conversations with him one comment he made in particular stuck with me. "When it is all said and done and everyone is paid something, even if I am left with nothing I want to be left with my integrity. I'm just not wired to walk away." Those are his words. A wise man once observed that the difficult circumstances of life *reveal* us; they don't *make* us. What's inside will come out.

David is a recent graduate of a local university and related to me the story of an incident that occurred late one Friday night in his co-ed dorm. He received a phone call from a friend who requested he come to a local bar and pick up 'Cindy' (name changed). David did not really know her; only that she lived with a group of girls down the hall and that they had quite a party reputation. He was informed Cindy was too drunk to walk, let alone drive, and they couldn't find any of her friends to get her home safely. David picked her up, delivered her safely to her dorm room and informed some girlfriends of hers down the hall to check in on her to be sure she was okay. David went back to his room and went to bed.

The next morning he got a knock on his door. It was Cindy. She asked if he was David. He said, "Yes," and she thanked him for taking care of her. Then she asked him another question, "Why didn't you take advantage of me? Everyone else takes advantage of me and I know you didn't." The boldness of the question surprised him at first, but then he realized she was both pleased and puzzled. He responded by telling her it was the right thing to do. He went on to tell her she needed to be safe, not taken advantage of. "I am a gentleman," he said, "and I treat ladies like ladies. I also happen to believe in God, and it honors Him when we treat people kindly."

Needless to say she was pretty impressed. They became friends and the story of his "chivalry" spread throughout the dorm. Breaking out this story in terms of the eight principles, I identify *reciprocity* (treating people the way you want to be treated), *fidelity* (faithfulness in the little things), *greatness* (great people serve people) and certainly, *responsibility* (to act on behalf of another). My point is not to sterilize the story by identifying the operative principles, but only to show that they work in the ordinariness of daily life. There is an inherent interplay with these principles. They don't operate as a single entity but in relationship with one another.

Tom is a personal injury attorney who has more business in his firm most of the time than he can handle. It all comes from word-of-mouth marketing— no advertising whatsoever. He made the decision to go on his own some years ago because he wanted to practice law in a manner where he could look at himself in the mirror each evening and feel good that he helped someone. That's actually one of his criteria for taking a case; will it truly help this person, or do they just want to gain dollars? He won't take the dollars-motivated cases. His other criteria is, "Can I win?" He said the two go hand in hand because if it's a legitimate injury case with real facts, the likelihood of winning is very good. *Reciprocity*, *responsibility* and *greatness*, at the very least, are observable characteristics of his practice. Remember Truett Cathy's comment that "if you take care of people, people will take care of you." Tom makes a good living and protects the uninformed and the vulnerable person at a time they need someone to be their advocate. As it should be, both are appropriately compensated.

There is indeed a "unity"" in all this. Unity is defined as a state of quality, accord, harmony and balance. Think about Tom, Rick, David, Denny, Lin, Jacob or any of the stories related in this book and the presence of the principle of unity is apparent. It looks different in each case, but it's there. This is the "stuff" of a meaningful life. When it's all said and done, this is what we want out of life—meaning. It doesn't "happen." It is the life lived consciously in light of what these eight principles look like in life, business and relationships that makes all the difference. Unity is a result, a consequence, of a choice to practice the principles.

CULTURES are LINES, NOT LIMITS

One of my friends is a former U.S. Ambassador to Ukraine. He kept a list of these eight principles on his desk by his computer monitor. He said he did this as a mental trigger before each appointment of the day, so he could make wiser decisions. He chose to live consciously; to make choices with intentionality.

Thinking truthfully and living consciously, as I commented earlier, fall under the category of those things in life that "say easy" but "do hard!" It's easy to say you are going to think truthfully and live consciously, but it's hard to actually do it on a moment by moment basis. The difficulty lies in the intentionality of it; the choice "to think outside the lines." The acknowledgment that there even are "lines" can be a major realization in itself.

In the last forty-eight hours I have met people from Peru, Italy, Switzerland, Spain, Columbia, Venezuela, Jamaica, Mexico and of course, Panama— as that is the location of my writing this day. The diversity of cultures living in one fifty-story condominium is striking. Tomorrow there will be more. Last month it was Europe.

Cultures are "lines." We live, think, observe and draw conclusions within them, and often we are totally unaware of it. It's in the "becoming aware" that we are able to begin to learn and make choices to live consciously both within those lines and in thoughtfully crossing the lines. A culture, however, is not definable only by national boundaries. I grew up in a small farming community in Northeastern Kansas in a blue collar family, attending a small school and a small church. In fact, about the only thing not small was my large family. After graduating from my small high school I attended a small college in large Chicago,

Illinois. Happily, my world has expanded widely and rapidly over the decades. Cultures exist within each other like a series of concentric circles expanding ever outward.

As diverse as we are as human beings it is my assumption that we all share one thing in common. We are created in the image of a Creator, and therein we find the unity. The diversity, however, is yet another reflection of the artful beauty of the creative genius of a Creator. Based on this premise of a Creator, I return to an earlier comment concerning our "hardwiring" as human beings. Though we may not share a culture in common, at our core we share the same "Manufacturer installed" need to live according to the shape of reality. We are hardwired to think and live truthfully and consciously, the consequence of which results in meaning. Life is meant to work a certain way and the eight principles, though not exhaustive, are reflective of the "shape" of reality.

Bahar is a well-educated young lady from Turkmenistan. She was a university student in Ukraine when I met her in 1999. I hired her to interpret for a business seminar we were conducting. Even though we have not seen each other since then, we have remained in touch over the years. She has continued to excel both academically and professionally. Early in our communication she commented that the experience of interpreting for us and engaging the team from the West via the seminar changed her life forever. She put it this way, "Before I met Global Leadership I never knew I was an individual human being and that I had my own personal choices. I can never be the same."

For many of us this is intuitive. Of course we have choices. Of course we are individuals. I would argue that if those thoughts are intuitive for you that it is because you grew up in a culture that is deeply influenced by a Judeo-Christian view of life and work.

The description of the world and how it works is not a religious description; it is reality. It's how things are made. There is not religious reality or secular reality. There is one objective reality. Gravity works the same for religious people and for non-religious people. It is one of many definitions of objective reality. It's how things were made, and it is the reality in which we all live. Reality has a "shape."

It is unfortunate that the institutional church has tended to hijack these universal human principles and attempted to present them as something religious or of the church. They are not. If indeed there is a Creator and the universe is His creative expression, then it is logical that the principles are indeed universal.

The eight principles/practices discussed in this book are some, not all, of those principles. They work because they are the shape of reality. To seek to make choices consistent with these principles is to think truthfully and live consciously. The stories related in this book are simply expressions of how some have chosen to answer the question, "What does this or that principle look like for me, lived out in my particular situations?"

A logical conclusion concerning the premise of a Creator is the fact that each of us is "creative" by nature. It is the thumbprint of the Creator; each of us is uniquely creative. None of us is exactly the same. You are one of a kind. No one is just like you. When you are gone, the original is gone. That makes you important and significant. The fact of your presence matters. You are not just one of a group; you are an individual, a creative and choice-making human being.

When you and I make choices we place a spin on history that was never before present. If, in fact, history is a collection of the consequences of the choices billions of people have made and continue to make, then it logically follows that your choices and my choices matter. Your choices make a difference. Your choices make history. When you are gone, your unique contribution to history is discontinued.

Germaine to our discussion of the shape of reality and the concepts of thinking truthfully and living consciously is this matter of creativity. Many of the stories related are expressions of how others have chosen to live out the principles. Each displays a creativity the other does not. It is often the case that when one considers this matter of creativity there is the natural tendency to think of the high profile and public expressions of creative people—the singer, performer, artist, architect of grand structures and the orator. However, creativity is not the exclusive domain of a few well-known people, but it is common to each of us. Creativity is often easier to identify in the obviously gifted and talented among us, but nevertheless, it is no less present within each and every one of us. It is the mark of the Creator.

How each of us goes about the business of living life consistent with the shape of reality requires creative choice-making. To "think truthfully" is to make the effort to realize there is a shape to reality. Things work a particular way because that's how they were made to work. "Living consciously" is the daily choice we make within the context of our creative uniqueness—to live out our lives with intentionality.

When she walks into just about any retail store someone behind the counter greets her by name. Anywhere she shops with any degree of regularity, there is a retailer friend she engages in conversation about their current life cares and concerns. It's not unusual for some of her lady friends to make playful fun of her for having friends everywhere she shops.

The Vietnamese lady who does her nails calls her "Mom." One particular Christmas she brought a tree, gifts, sweet breads and cookies to the nail shop and gave it to her manicurist so her two little girls would have a proper celebration. The "office supply" store she frequents goes out of their way to provide the best possible service they can. When she walks into the store, they light up and greet her by name. I recall a situation when she was walking with some difficulty due to a foot injury. The manager took her list of needed supplies and went around the store, collecting it all for her.

For many of the past Christmas seasons I have known her to bake seventy plus loaves of Pumpkin Chocolate Chip bread. She distributed them to retail stores, the UPS delivery man, the mail carrier, neighbors and a local restaurant. The restaurant alone received more than forty of the loaves because she wanted to be sure everyone got a gift—from the owners to the table cleaners, servers, cashiers and cooks. It has also happened that she has gone to another lady's home to assist her with decorating ideas, getting the house organized, closets cleaned out and drawers straightened as the younger mom was feeling overwhelmed by life.

It is not unusual for her to spend hours on the phone or in person with another woman discussing child-raising, relationships or a current problematic adolescent issue. In her younger years she mentored college girls, and in her later years she gave leadership to an organization of 200 young mothers who wanted guidance in the task of balancing the demands of family life and professional life.

If you are reading carefully you will hear the unity of some of the principles at play. She is a "homemaker," mother, grandmother and wife. I know these things about her and a lot more because I have been privileged to spend more than four decades in a marriage relationship with her. She never ceases to amaze me and challenges me to be a better person. She is an extraordinary, ordinary person. She is a uniquely, creative, choice-making person . . . just like the rest of us. Thinking truthfully and wishing to live consciously she creatively makes choices to live it out in the dailyness of life. It's a choice. It's intentional. And it's a lot of fun!

The stories you have read are not intended to brag on someone else nor to necessarily suggest you imitate them. They are intended to be illustrative, only in the hopes that one or two would provoke both thought and ideas we would choose to make a practice. After all, there is no one else on planet earth quite like you. You are unique. You are not just one of the group. Each of us is living a life and therefore, writing our own story. Write your unique story with intentionality. There *will* be a story—whether by intention or by default.

Think truthfully, live consciously.

The consequences are profoundly rewarding and the possibilities are as endless as creativity itself.

About the Author

Jesse James
Founder and CEO: Global Leadership, Inc.

Jesse's experience in the former Soviet Union began in 1992 as an educational consultant for the Russian Education Federation. He traveled extensively throughout Russia, Ukraine and Belarus leading teams of American educators to more than 40 cities. After 31 years on the Staff of Cru he founded the nonprofit organization, Global Leadership, Inc.. In addition, he cofounded a manufacturing export business operating out of Kiev, Ukraine.

Jesse's background is primarily in the field of education and leadership development. He did his undergraduate work at Moody College and graduate studies at Dallas Theological Seminary. He, also, serves on the board of the Francis A. Schaeffer Foundation based in Gryon, Switzerland. Dr. Schaeffer understood that what a person believes influences the way he acts in history and individual situations. This philosophy deeply informs Jesse's view of his life and work.

Jesse and his wife Carolynn make their home together in the Atlanta, Georgia area. Their 4 children and 10 grandchildren also live in the greater Atlanta area.

Jesse James

Founder and CEO

GLOBAL LEADERSHIP, Inc.

6685 Tulip Garden Way

Alpharetta, GA 30004

jesse@globalleadership.us